THESE ARE OUR BODIES

FOR PRIMARY

Church Publishing
NEW YORK

PARTICIPANT BOOK

Scripture from the *New Revised Standard Version Bible (NRSV)* © 1989 by the Division of Christian Education of the National Council of Churches of Christ in the USA. Used by permission.

Scripture quotations from the CEB used with permission. All rights reserved. Common English Bible, Copyright 2011.

A catalog record of this book is available from the Library of Congress.

Church Publishing Incorporated
19 East 34th Street
New York, NY 10016

Cover design by: Jennifer Kopec, 2 Pug Design
Typeset by: Progressive Publishing Services

ISBN-13: 978-0-89869-057-6 (pbk.)

Printed in the United States of America

CONTENTS

INTRODUCTION

Welcome to *These Are Our Bodies*!

Jesus said, "Let the little children come to me." This class is for children like you, who are learning and growing. It is a place to help you feel God's love for you. This is a class for you and your parents to learn more about your body and more about God. You will play some games and learn new things, too.

Get ready to have some fun!

Jenny Beaumont and Abbi Long

GOD
KNOWS ME

The gatekeeper opens the gate for him,
and the sheep hear his voice.
He calls his own sheep by name
and leads them out.
I am the good shepherd.
I know my own and my own know me,
just as the Father knows me
and I know the Father.
—John 10:3, 14

Prayer

Thank you God for keeping me near to you and for caring for me. I know that you love my family and me. Help me to learn more about you and the special way that you created all of me. *Amen*.

Draw a picture that shows you and Jesus together.

Today we learned about each other, Jesus' love for each of us, and our family's love for us. You are loved!

THE STORY OF ME BOOK

Write down parts of your story . . .

My Beginning

The Story of My Name

I Am a Gift from God

My Baptism

Me Now

WITH YOUR FAMILY AT HOME

The story of the Good Shepherd helps us remember that God knows us by name. Use the sheep below to think about the parable again from John 10.

Can you give them each a name?

Who does God know by name in your family?

What are the names of some friends that God knows by name?

With crayons or markers, add to the pictures of the sheep. Draw some grass or ground. Add in the sky.

Jesus knows us by name.

Prayer

The LORD bless you and keep you; the LORD make his face to shine upon you, and be gracious to you; the LORD lift up his countenance upon you, and give you peace.

—Numbers 6:24–26

I AM
LOVED

"I give you a new commandment:
Love each other.
Just as I have loved you,
so you also must love each other.
This is how everyone will know
that you are my disciples,
when you love each other."
—John 13: 34–35 (CEB)

Prayer

Dear God, thank you for loving me and for sending Jesus and giving us a new commandment: To love each other, as you have loved us. Help me to love my friends and myself, too. *Amen*.

BLESSINGS

We are going to make a blessing prayer.

Here is an example of a Blessing Card that is for your mom:

MOM is kind and loving.
Thank you God for my Mom.

Who do you want to bless? Put their name here or draw their picture.

Choose two adjectives to describe the person. Here are some examples:

Loving	Enthusiastic
Kind	Joyful
Gentle	Thoughtful
Prayerful	Smart
Generous	Selfless
Hopeful	Faithful
Grateful	

Write your own words here:

You may want to draw something to remind you of the person. Draw some things that describe your parent, family member, or friend.

Draw words or a picture that tell about your family member. Write some of those words here:

Once you have two to five words, it's time to create your Blessing Card.

My Blessing Card is for _____.

_____ is _____
_____ and
_____.

Thank you God for _____.

WITH YOUR FAMILY AT HOME

The story of Jesus and the little children reminds us that Jesus loved all people, even very young people. He welcomed them with his hands wide open.

Trace one of your hands on the next page. You can also trace one of your parents' hands on top of your hand.

Use a different color crayon or marker so you can see the different hands.

Draw the faces or bodies of all the people you think Jesus welcomes. You can draw yourself. You can draw your friends at church or school. You can draw other children and people in the world.

Below your picture write this message: **Jesus Welcomes Everyone!**

Prayer

Loving and awesome God, thank you for my family. Thank you for giving me people to love and people who love me. Help us to remember that we have all been blessed by your grace. Stay close to us, and keep us close to each other as we learn and grow. *Amen*.

Write or draw your own prayer.

GOD MADE ME

O LORD, you have searched me and known me.
You know when I sit down and when I rise up;
    you discern my thoughts from far away.
You search out my path and my lying down,
    and are acquainted with all my ways.
Even before a word is on my tongue,
    O LORD, you know it completely.
You hem me in, behind and before,
    and lay your hand upon me.
Even the darkness is not dark to you;
    the night is as bright as the day,
    for darkness is as light to you.

For it was you who formed my inward parts;
you knit me together in my mother's womb.
I praise you, for I am fearfully and
wonderfully made.
Wonderful are your works;
that I know very well.
My frame was not hidden from you,
when I was being made in secret,
intricately woven in the depths of the earth.
Your eyes beheld my unformed substance.
In your book were written
all the days that were formed for me,
when none of them as yet existed.
How weighty to me are your thoughts, O God!
How vast is the sum of them!
—Psalm 139:1–5, 12–17

Prayer

Thank you, God, for always being with me. You look for me and find me. You lead me to places to play and keep me safe. You know even when I stand up and when I sit down again. When I look around, I see what you have created. Help me to be still and know you are the Lord.[1] Thank you, God. *Amen*.

1 Adapted from Psalm 46 and Psalm 139.

Think about the things we use our body for: hugging, smiling, tickling, running, cuddling, smelling, and more. Think about what you are good at doing or things that you enjoy. Draw those things on the body below to remind how we use our body with the gifts God have given us. Look on the next page for some suggestions.

These objects help our bodies do things:

A ball for catching or kicking
Glasses for reading
A pot and spoon for cooking
Dancing shoes for dancing
Paintbrushes for painting
Book for reading
Instruments for playing
Pencils or markers for drawing
Sneakers for running

What other things can you think of for using the gifts God gave you?

I AM GRATEFUL FOR . . .

Think about the amazing things that your body can do and the things you love to do. Write down something about your body you are grateful for. Also write down why you are grateful for it.

I am grateful for _____
because _____.

WITH YOUR FAMILY AT HOME

Psalm 139 reminds us that God made us—inside and out. It reminds us that God knows about our lives; even things we think are a secret. Talk about the game "Hide and Seek."

What are the rules to the game? Write down those rules here:

1.

2.

3.

4.

Draw three places you might hide in a game of "Hide and Seek."

Talk about Psalm 139 with your family using the questions below.

Can you hide from God?

Can you go somewhere that God's love cannot reach?

Talk about hiding from God or God's love with your family.

Why might we try to hide from God's love?

Will God come and seek us if we try to hide?

Circle an answer for each of these questions. Talk about your answers together.

1. Is there anything we can do to make God love us less?

    Yes   No   I don't know

2. Is there anything we can say to make God love us less?

    Yes   No   I don't know

3. Is there anywhere we can go where God's love won't seek us out?

    Yes   No   I don't know

Thank you, Creator God, who made me all of me—inside and out! *Amen.*

MORE IDEAS FOR AT HOME

After Parent Session 4

Together as a family, fill in these blanks with your own words.

God loves _____; that means all of _____.
Your spirit and your body are _____
_____.

God made a way for families to have _____. Our bodies are perfectly created to make _____.

God made each of us uniquely different and _____. We are made in the image of _____.

Write your own family's faith connections here:

After Parent Session 5

As a family, talk about some words you need to know about human bodies. If you want, make a list of ten words here that all of you want to learn more about.

Words to know about:

1.

2.

3.

4.

5.

6.

7.

8.

9.

10.

Now that you have made a list, talk about those words. Talk about a way to find out information that is factual and true.

Ask yourself, where can I find out what a word means? You can add more words later if you want.

After Parent Session 8

A loving affirmation makes the heart, mind, and body feel good. Practice writing words that talk about goodness, love, acceptance, and a joy-filled life. Try filling in these blanks with your family. After filling them in with words that say how good something is, try saying them aloud to each other. You could also write them on paper and put them around the house as reminders. Challenge each other to say these kind words as often as you see the reminders.

My body is _____.

Your body is _____.

I love my _____.

I love your _____.

When you are around, I feel _____.

You have great _____.

I have great _____.

My _____ are beautiful.

My _____ is amazing.

After Parent Session 9

Using the following secret code, uncover with your parents a phrase you need to know.

A = 20   H = 11   O = 25   V = 22

B = 15   I = 17   P = 16   W = 19

C = 1   J = 21   Q = 12   X = 10

D = 3   K = 13   R = 26   Y = 24

E = 14   L = 5   S = 8   Z = 4

F = 6   M = 2   T = 23

G = 9   N = 18   U = 7

15 25 3 24

20 7 23 25 18 25 2 24

With your parents, talk about what you discovered. What does it mean? Why is it important?